Totally Fun Things to Do with Your CAT

Maxine Rock

Illustrated by Ed Shems

John Wiley & Sons, Inc.

New York • Chichester • Weinheim • Brisbane • Singapore • Toronto

Copyright © 1998 by Maxine Rock.
Illustrations copyright © 1998 by Ed Shems.
Published by John Wiley & Sons, Inc.
Design and production by Navta Associates, Inc.

The publisher and the author have made every reasonable effort to ensure that the experiments and activities in the book are safe when conducted as instructed but assume no responsibility for any damage caused or sustained while performing the experiments or activities in this book. Parents, guardians, and/or teachers should supervise young readers who undertake the experiments and activities in this book.

Library of Congress Cataloging-in-Publication Data
Rock, Maxine A.
    Totally fun things to do with your cat / Maxine Rock; illustrated by Ed Shems.
        p. cm.
    Summary: Discusses how to choose and take care of a pet cat and describes various fun activities to share with and toys to make for your cat.
    ISBN 0-471-19575-8 (pbk. : alk. paper)
    1. Games for cats—Juvenile literature. [1. Cats. 2. Games for cats. 3. Pets.]
    I. Shems, Ed, ill. II. Title.
    SF446.7.R63 1998   97-49027
    636.8'083—dc21   CIP
Printed in the United States of America
10 9 8 7 6 5 4 3 2 1

This book is dedicated to Kitty
(alias Kitty My Darling) and
to her favorite human pets,
Lauren Rock and Michael Rock

—Maxine Rock

❧ Contents ❧

Introduction

This is a book about having fun with your cat. In order to have fun, however, you must choose a healthy, happy pet and learn how to keep her that way! This introduction will give you the basics. For more information, consult the many pet care books available.

Of course, your cat may be a male, but the cats in this book will be referred to as "her" or "she" just to make things easier.

Health and Safety

The Healthy Cat

Pedigree or plain old stray, you should pick a cat in obvious good health. Here's how to tell:

- A healthy cat is alert, curious, and eager to interact with a friendly, interested human. Chances are if a cat is playful, she's not sick.

- A healthy cat has thick, shiny fur, with no bald or scruffy patches.

- Check her ears. If there's brown gunk inside, or if the cat is scratching her ears so much the fur is worn off, she may have ear mites. These are easily cured with ear drops, though, so you don't necessarily have to pass up this cat if she is otherwise healthy.

- Look into the cat's eyes. Just before you become hypnotized, see that the cat has bright, dry eyes and there is little if any mucus around them.

- The cat's nose should also be free of discharge, and it should be smooth, not cracked.

- The cat's lips should be clean and free of saliva, and her mouth should be pink.

- Don't bring fleas home with the cat. If she's scratching, have the pet shop or humane center person "deflea" her with powder or spray.

- Cats can get colds or the flu, so make sure she isn't sneezing.

- If the cat you want is over nine weeks old, make sure she has been vaccinated against feline enteritis and feline leukemia. Both are fatal cat diseases.

Take your new pet for a full checkup at the veterinarian. Make sure she gets any shots she needs. Even if she's healthy, a checkup makes sure she stays that way.

3

Cat Safety

Some people feel that cats should be kept indoors at all times to ensure their safety. Others allow cats to remain outside at least some of the time. If you and your parents decide to keep the cat indoors, you may want to consider a procedure called "declawing," which will remove the cat's claws so she can't damage furniture or rugs. An outdoor cat needs her claws to climb and escape if she is being pursued by a dog or by another cat.

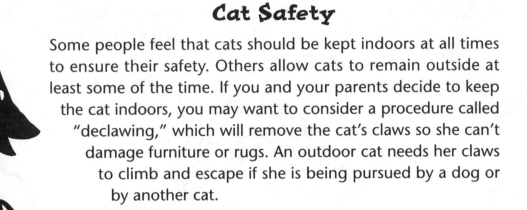

Avoiding the "Ouch!" Factor

Y ou don't have to sport scratched-up hands or arms as a consequence of having fun with your cat. But cats do express affection by biting and clawing. It's okay when they do this with other cats, whose thick fur and loose skin protect them. But you (hopefully) do not have thick fur and loose skin, so here's what you need to know to protect your precious flesh:

- Use bare hands only to stroke and calm your cat. When playing, use toys and encourage her to bite them, not you. If you want to play with your cat using your hands, wear gloves.

- It's inevitable: she will dig in at some point. Steel yourself. Don't yell or pull or jerk your hand away because her claws or teeth won't have time to disengage; just stop what you're doing. Gently push the cat's feet forward, not away. Pushing forward is what disengages the claws. Pushing away just hooks them deeper into skin.

- Refocus your cat's attention on a toy, not on your hand.

- If she persists in wanting to show her affection this way, ignore her. That is far more effective than yelling, hitting, or having to zoom off in an ambulance. Eventually, your cat will realize that claws on skin is a no-no.

Litter Boxes

If your cat stays outdoors, she won't need a litter box. If she's an indoor cat, or sometimes comes indoors, she will need a litter box so she won't soil the house. Litter boxes are usually made of plastic and are available for a minimal amount in any pet shop. Fill the box with store-bought litter and put it in a quiet corner where the cat has as much privacy as possible.

Many cats will use the litter box at once, if you show it to them and do not disturb them when they want to use it. You can litter-train a young cat by watching to see when she squats. That's the time to gently lift her up and put her in the box. Put newspapers under and around the box. If she uses the newspaper, simply put her in the box as soon as possible thereafter. Never scold, shout, or hit your cat while training. Punishment for soiling will not encourage her to do better; it will only frighten and confuse her. Your best training tool for a cat—as for any animal—is patience and love. Just keep trying, and your cat will use the litter box because she wants to please you, and also because it's a natural urge for cats to cover up their leavings.

Neutering

Both male and female cats should be neutered to avoid bringing unwanted kittens into the world. (Male cats are neutered, females are spayed, and in referring to both or either, you can use the generic term "neutered".) Male cats won't roam if they are neutered, and an unspayed female cat can be responsible for 20,000 descendants in just five years! To keep your pet safer, and to make sure you don't contribute to kitten overpopulation, it is kind to neuter your cat. It is *not* true that a female cat should have one litter before spaying. Spay or neuter your cat at six months of age.

Picking the Perfect Cat

Some people think cats are self-absorbed furballs who pay attention to humans only when it's time for a snack. That's true.

Others believe cats are soft and adorable, funny and playful, and capable of great love for their human owners. That's true, too.

Huh?

Don't get too confused. Cats are *complicated.* When your cat is in the mood to be stuck-up and ignore you, she will do just that. When she wants to play or snuggle, your cat won't take no for an answer. She'll find you, plop down on your lap, and look up at you with her big, round eyes until you stop what you're doing and agree to have some fun.

All cats are different, of course, but the capacity to be both sulky and loving seems to be built into cat DNA. You never really know what a cat is going to do, or how she will react. That's what keeps life with a cat from being dull.

THE RIGHT WAY TO PICK UP A CAT

There's a right way and a wrong way to pick up a cat. Picking her up the right way will make her feel comfortable and secure. Picking her up the wrong way will hurt her, frighten her, and may cause her to avoid you.

Don't grab your cat around the middle, because that chokes off her air supply. Don't pick her up under the armpits, because her legs dangle and the weight of her body will pull down—that hurts.

Just slip one hand under her chest, and the other hand under her hindquarters. Gently bring her to your chest, supporting the full weight of her body with the hand that is under her hindquarters. By holding your cat close to your chest, she won't feel as if she is "hanging in space."

Always leave the cat's front paws free, so she can use them to balance. Cats hate being grabbed by their front paws. If your cat struggles, cries, or indicates that she is unhappy being picked up, let her down at once and try again later.

Right way

Wrong way

Kitten or Older Cat?

Kittens are cute. They can also act pretty nuts. They roll, scoot, jump, and in general act like they've got ants in their kitten pants. Older cats have usually acquired some feline dignity and aren't as likely to turn your house into a shambles. Both kittens and older cats like to play, although a kitten will play longer, harder, and crazier than an adult cat. Your cat's personality (which is pretty individual) is really more important than its age. Kittens grow up very fast. If you select a kitten, do not remove her from her mother's care until she is at least eight weeks of age.

What Breed?

Does it make any difference what breed of cat you buy or adopt? There are at least 100 different breeds of cats, but only about eight percent of the cats people own in the United States are purebreds. The common cats most of us adopt are descended from the breed of British Shorthairs; if they have any breed name at all, it's American Shorthair. These "alley cats" come in a wide variety of colors and patterns, and their personalities are as varied as their looks.

Dogs were bred by humans to perform certain functions, such as being watchdogs, and the personalities of dogs usually fit the jobs that they were bred to do. For example, German shepherds make

SOME POPULAR CAT BREEDS

Turkish Van Likes to swim, and may do laps in the pool with you!

Ragdoll So easygoing that it flops around like a rag doll when you pick it up.

Persian Big eyes, gorgeous fur, and an appealing disposition.

Maine Coon Looks like a raccoon, and is also handy with its front paws.

Scottish Fold Ears fold back, making it look like a teddy bear. Intelligent.

Siamese Graceful and sociable, with big blue eyes and a loud meow.

Abyssinian Regal, slender, and loves humans. Learns tricks easily.

Tonkinese Friendly, acrobatic, and enjoys toys. Invents games. May play fetch.

good guard dogs because they were bred for that job; their personalities tend to make them wary of strangers and highly motivated to keep their owners from danger. Cats, however, were bred mostly for body shape, color, and type of fur. Their personalities do vary somewhat according to breed, but cats are individuals and each one has her own distinct charm.

Sometimes the names of breeds reflect a cat's physical characteristics, such as Angora, because they have long, soft hair; Calico, for the pretty patches of black, red, and white they display; and Siamese, because they look so exotic. Although you will be swayed by how a cat looks, also pay careful attention to her personality. A friendly, mild-mannered, and playful alley cat will make you a lot happier than a stunning pedigree cat with a personality like a snooty princess.

How a Cat Picks You

You probably think you're totally in charge of selecting the cat. Right? Wrong. The cat also selects *you*.

You will be drawn to a particular cat by the way she looks and how she acts. A healthy, happy cat will not only be pretty, but will be interested in you and curious to see if you are a fun-loving human.

In addition to spending time with the cat and observing how readily she plays with you, another good way to find out if she's frisky is

Guess what? Thirty percent of the people in the United States live with cats. That's the second-highest percentage of cat owners in the world. Australia is first, where 33 percent of the people own cats.

to wiggle a handkerchief or some yarn on the floor in front of her. The playful animal will bounce over to investigate and swat, leap, roll around, or otherwise try to initiate a game.

An interested, healthy cat will also perk up her ears and look in your direction if you call to her. How do you call a cat? Try, "Here, Kitty!" for starters. (If she comes, it might be because she feels sorry for you, since you're dumb enough to think her name is Kitty.)

The curious cat, who thinks it's fun to crawl up the legs of your jeans, is checking to see how playful *you* are. The cat wandering over to sniff your hand is deciding whether to pronounce you fit to be a possible owner.

The cat rubbing her head against you is both inviting you to pet her and "marking" you as her territory.

> **Tip**
>
> Cats normally live 12 to 14 years, but with luck and excellent care some cats stick around a lot longer. A calico in Atlanta named Kitty My Darling lived to 22 years. The oldest cat on record was Puss, a tabby who lived in England. Puss was 38 when he died in 1939. Regular veterinary care, an excellent diet, and plenty of love will help your cat live as long as possible.

Each of these cat characters will then conduct a thorough interview for the job of keeping her supplied with great food and pillows for about 12 years, which is the normal life span for a cat.

The interview consists of:

- Tasting your clothing

- Chewing a little of your hair

- Sniffing to make sure you haven't been in contact with another cat—or, heaven forbid, a dog—for a while

- Rubbing against you some more

- Deciding if you're enough of a sucker to obey her completely.

Okay. The cat has decided you'll do. Take her home.

What's in a Name?

Figuring out the names of some cat breeds can be a real challenge. The Burmese cat is called Malayan in the United States. In Great Britain, the Platinum Malayan is called the Lilac Burmese. Burmese and Malayan are supposed to be the same breed, except the Malayan was developed in the United States and the Burmese came from Great Britain in 1969.

Despite all this, the word "cat" seems surprisingly similar in several different languages. In German, it's *katze.* The French word for cat is *chat.* Cat in Spanish is *gato,* and Italian, it is *gatta.* Russians call their domestic felines *kot.*

In the United States, cats have many nicknames. A cat can be called a kitty, feline, pussy, tabby, Tom, or tomcat (male). An old-fashioned name for cats is *grimalkin.* It means "elderly woman," or "old female cat."

Naming your own cat can be fun, and many people come up with pretty far-out names for their cats like Moonpie, Witchcraft, Celestial Navigation, Kinky, Percival, Mad Max, and Pooch-Biter (you can guess what that cat did for a hobby). A recent survey taken in America by a cat magazine shows that Tiger and Samantha are the nation's favorite cat names.

The late comedian George Burns had a cat named Willie. Burns said he gave the cat that name because "When you told the cat what to do, it was always a question of *will he,* or won't he."

Chapter 1

Getting Familiar with Your Feline

It's fun just bringing your cat home and watching her snoop around, getting familiar with your house, yard, family, and other pets, if you have them. But don't let her get too familiar with a small caged bird or an unprotected fish.

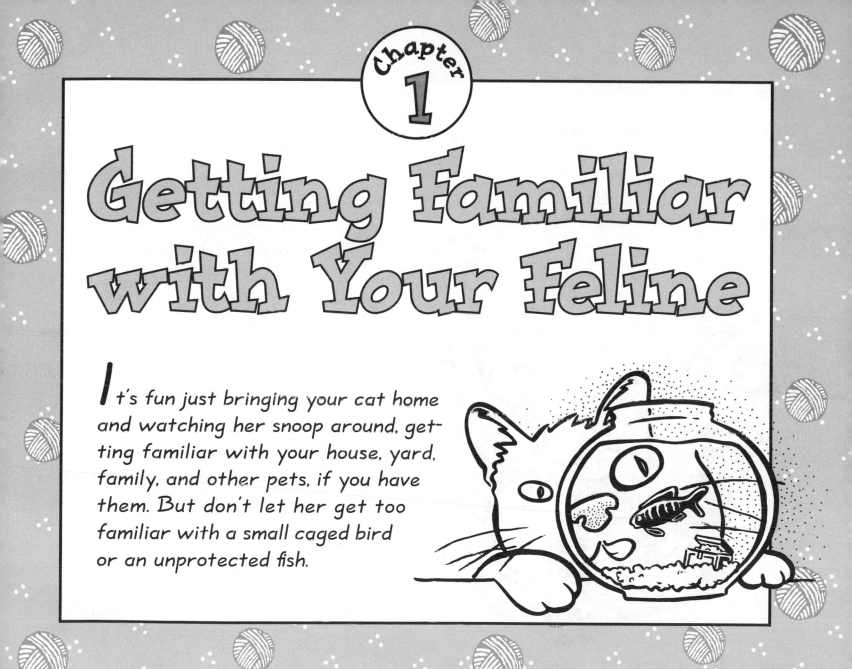

Cats are naturally curious. They explore *everything*, and like to crawl into warm places to scope them out or just curl up for a nap. So keep the oven door closed. Peek inside the washing machine and dryer before using them.

The most common cats in the world are nonpedigree cats—mixtures of several breeds. The term for a domestic, nonpedigree cat is "Moggy."

Look under the car before it is started. Make sure your cat isn't snoozing in the wrong spot.

Your cat will need time alone to sniff around the house and establish her "territory." This means she will decide where she wants to sit (in the most comfortable chair); where she'll sleep (probably in your bed, on your pillow, or even on your head); and what food she wants (everything). Okay. Now it's clear that she is the boss.

Saying Hello to a Cat

Good cat manners demand that you never just reach down, grab the cat, and pick it up. First, you have to say hello. How would you feel if someone much bigger than you hauled you up into the air without at least saying "Hi"?

Cats enjoy meeting people, if they are relaxed, fed, and in a good mood (this goes for both cats and people). Teach every person in your family the proper way to greet your new cat, at least for the first time:

1 Lean down, with your hands behind your back, and face the cat.

2 Stick out your nose. Yes, that's the way a cat says hello—nose first.

3 The cat will stretch up to greet you with her nose.

Tip

Don't plop down next to a sleeping cat, or startle her awake. Never run after a cat who is trying to escape from you. Never corner a cat. If she hisses, retreat. Trying to say hello to a frightened cat just invites a cat-astrophe.

4 Now you can put out your hand. Don't pet the cat; just brush your hand very lightly over the tips of the fur on her back. You're not really touching her— just sort of skimming the fur. If the cat wants you to pet her, she'll arch upward to meet your hand.

Chow Time!

Just feeding a cat is fun because the cat will get so enthusiastic about chow time that she'll run to you, curl around your legs, look up, and meow with anticipation. Some cats like to "dance" on their hind legs before dinner, and others roll, twirl, or leap up to wherever you're preparing the food. Here are a few mealtime tips:

- While a very hungry cat might gobble down her meal, most well-fed cats are nibblers. Put down wet (canned) or dry (usually comes in bags) food. Dry food is better, but many cats prefer wet food; you may want to alternate. Let the cat pick around at her food for about 30 or 40 minutes, then remove the food.

- Keep the cat's water dish clean and filled with fresh water. It's a good idea to change the water a few times a day.

- Your cat likes human food? Okay. After she eats some cat food, you can share small bits of meat, toast, vegetables, spaghetti, and pizza. *No chicken bones! They shred, and can choke a cat.*

- Cats love tuna. Once they taste its strong flavor, some cats won't eat anything else! To avoid having a cat who is a tuna monster, don't give it to her at all. Tuna can even cause health problems in some cats.

The ancestor of all domestic cats was probably a striped yellow animal called the African wild cat. Early humans quickly domesticated dogs, but cats stayed wild until people became farmers, stored grain, and needed cats to hunt grain-stealing mice. The farmers put out food for wild cats to lure them into domesticity.

Introduce Me, Please

If you want two pets, it's best to get them both at the same time. That way, they enter your home as equals. And if you want two cats, or a dog and a cat, getting them both while they're very young makes it easy for them to grow up together and become good friends.

But what if you're trying to introduce a new cat to one that's been around for a while, or trying to get an older cat and dog to be friends? It can be done, even if the new arrival and the established pet are wary of one another, or even snarl and hiss at first.

Introducing Two Cats to One Another

1 Put the cats in separate rooms for several days. Let them hear and smell each other under a closed door, or through a door propped open just an inch or two.

2 Feed the cats at the same time, right at the place where the door opens, so they can see each other eating.

3 After the cats get used to sniffing, hearing, and peeking at one another, open the door a little more. You may want to introduce a toy at this point, to see if the cats want to bat it back and forth to one another.

4 When you finally open the door all the way, stay close enough to remove one cat if it gets frightened or hostile.

5 If the cats fight, ask your veterinarian about other methods or even medications that may make the process go more smoothly. It often takes patience and encouragement to complete the introduction.

Introducing a Cat and a Dog

1 Put the dog in a carrying case, wire enclosure, or other secure corral where the animals can see one another clearly, but not touch. Let the cat investigate nearby. This lets the animals get used to one another without endangering the cat. This process will also take at least several days.

2 When you let the dog out, keep the dog on a leash until cat and dog become friends and you're *positive* the dog won't rush to or grab the cat.

3 Keep calm. Act as if you expect them to get along. Both animals will pick up on your attitude.

Chapter 2

Talking to Your Cat

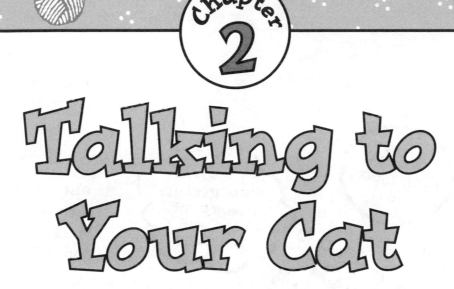

Cats have good hearing, and they love certain sounds such as low, gentle music and your voice when it is soothing and soft. They *hate jangling noises, loud horns and sirens,* and voices that are shrill and angry.

Here are the human sounds cats enjoy most:

- whispers
- anything said in a sing-song voice
- chuckles and soft laughs
- a gently spoken falsetto, such as you would use with an infant (Example: "Oh, you're such a sweet, pretty, intelligent cat!")
- your soft breathing when you're asleep

Here are household sounds cats enjoy most:

- the can opener (it often means her food is on the way)

- rustles and crinkly sounds, such as the one made when you crumple up a wad of paper into a ball

- doors opening softly (cats are curious)

- small things being scooted or rolled across a hard floor (also makes the cat curious)

Sounds Cats Love

Are You Listening?

A cat who loves you will perk up her ears at the sound of your voice, look in your direction, and probably come even before you call her. Cats listen to people they like (if they're in the mood, that is). If someone a cat doesn't like comes into the room, the cat will either jump to a high spot where the person can't reach her, or leave.

Here are ways to talk to your cat, in her language, as much as that's possible:

MEOW to your cat, and she will probably meow back. You're both saying hello.

TRILL by holding your tongue down and vibrating it. Nobody knows what that means, but cats seem to like it . . .

PURSE your lips into a kiss and repeat very rapidly. That means "come here."

OHHH, OHHH, OHHH repeated softly is a soothing sound that calms your cat and draws her to you.

Here are ways the cat talks to you:

MEOW! "I'm starving! What is there to eat in this joint?"

HOWL! Sounds like "Yeowww!" It means "You just stepped on my tail, you jerk!"

PURR "I see you're trying to take a nap on the sofa. You don't mind if I lie down right here on your tummy, do you?"

MEW, MEW, MEW "I'm so adorable, how could you blame me for breaking that vase? I'm just an innocent little kitty!"

Silly superstition: Cats are jealous of babies, and try to smother them while they're asleep. Fact: Cats are curious about everything, including babies. So a cat may jump into the crib to check out the new arrival, but she will not hurt an infant.

Playing with Sounds

Here are some sound experiments to try on your cat:

- Do you have a piano? Your cat may perch on the seat next to you as you play, or find a spot on top of the piano where she can look down at your fingers. Cats are delighted by the finger movements of piano playing, and some cats even jump or walk on the keys to try to reproduce the sound or mimic what you were doing.

- If you play the violin, your cat will follow the movement of the bow across the strings, or try to swat at the strings.

- With a flute or recorder, your cat may follow the movements up and down, and purr or meow in harmony.

- Wad up a piece of aluminum foil and send it skittering along the floor. Your cat will be attracted by the crinkly sound.

- Roll wax paper into a ball, and secure it with string. Pull it along a bare floor. Your cat will react to the sound of the paper on the floor.

- Tear off a piece of cellophane or plastic wrap and roll it in your hands. The cat will try to see what's making that funny noise in your hand. (Put away the foil, string, and plastic wrap when you're done. You don't want your cat playing with these items when she's alone; she may swallow parts of them and choke.)

- Drop uncooked green beans, one by one, on a bare floor. The cat will "attack" each one, excited by the sound.

- Get two or more walnuts and roll them across the floor. Your cat will run after the one that makes the loudest noise.

- Any toy with a soft whirr, probably one with wheels, will entice your cat to leap on it, especially if you pull it along slowly, then speed up, then slow down again. That's how something alive might act. Your cat will pretend that the toy is alive, and she is stalking it.

When your cat rubs her chin, forehead, or tail against a door or fence post, she is establishing her territory. Cats stake out rooms, yards, or entire neighborhoods as their special places. The cat who "owns" the most places is respected as dominant by other cats. When a cat rubs against you, she is saying, "I own you."

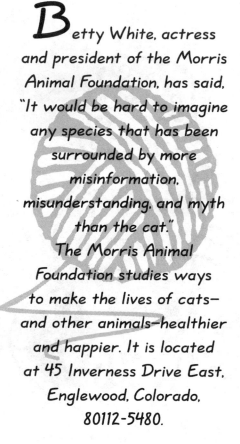

Betty White, actress and president of the Morris Animal Foundation, has said, "It would be hard to imagine any species that has been surrounded by more misinformation, misunderstanding, and myth than the cat." The Morris Animal Foundation studies ways to make the lives of cats—and other animals—healthier and happier. It is located at 45 Inverness Drive East, Englewood, Colorado, 80112-5480.

Reading Cat Body Language

Cats communicate with every part of their bodies. To understand what your cat is saying, pay attention to her eyes, ears, paws, and position.

Eyes

Very round "I'm looking at something interesting," or "I'm seeing something that scares me."

Narrow, blinking slowly "I'm content."

Very wide open "Open the door!" "Gimme the food!" or "I'm really mad!"

Ears

Forward "What's that sound?"

Up, pointed sideways "I can't decide if I want to investigate or take a nap."

Flat, down "I'm confused," or "I'm angry."

Flat, sideways "Umm, that feels good. Scratch me some more."

Paws

Patting gently, nails in "Are you awake yet?"

Jumps stiffly, legs straight "Maybe if I jump on you, you'll wake up!"

Kneads you, just before lying down "You make a pretty good pillow, but I'll just mash down this little lump here . . . "

Curls paws as she walks or rests "I'm feeling pretty good. Don't you think I'm a pretty neat cat?"

Position

Curled in a crouch, fur fluffed up "I'm cold," or "I'm mad."

Curled in a ball, tail over eyes "It's cold, but I fell asleep anyway."

On her back, legs extended "I'm hot."

Crouching, leaning forward "I'm just waiting for that bug to get a little closer, and then I'll pounce . . ."

Back arched, tail up "Pet me, please."

Back arched, tail up, fur up "I'm scared!" or "Watch out; I'm ready to attack!"

29

WHAT DOES BRUSHING SAY TO YOUR CAT?

Cats love being brushed. To them, it means you care enough to spend quiet time stroking and petting them. Brushing helps maintain a cat's health . . . and it certainly is good for your relationship. Cats are self-groomers, but brushing makes sure their fur doesn't mat and removes loose hair, dust, and dirt. It also distributes natural oils throughout your cat's coat, and prevents furballs, which can form in a cat's stomach and make her sick. Another plus: daily brushing helps to keep shedding under control.

Here are some tips on the proper way to brush your cat:

- Use a special cat brush made for your cat's type of fur (long or short). There are also special "grooming mitts" that you can use instead of a brush.

- Start at the cat's head and gently brush all the way to her tail.

- If the cat cries or seems uncomfortable, she may have a skin irritation. (Have your veterinarian check this out.)

- If the area around your cat's eyes is wet, wipe it lightly with a soft, damp cloth.

- Always be gentle, and brush slowly. Keep your voice low.

- Brush at the same time each day. Soon, your cat will present herself at that time for a brushing session!

- If your cat doesn't want to be brushed on a certain day, skip it!

Smarty-Cat

How to Judge Your Cat's I.Q.

Do cats think? Are they smart? Yes, and yes. Here's a fun way to tell if you have a feline Einstein or a reject from "Beavis and Butt-head":

1 Show your cat a jug full of milk.

2 While she watches, open the bottle and give her a little. (Some cats get an upset stomach from dairy products, so restrict your pet's intake of milk and other dairy items. Even if she tolerates them well, large amounts of such items aren't good for her.)

3 Seal the jug tightly and pretend to leave the room.

Don't go too far; just find a spot nearby where you can spy on the cat, but where she can't see *you*. Wait about one or two minutes, so she really thinks she's alone.

*A*mazing! Cats really can find their way home if you take them far away. They use a navigation system similar to that of birds: They detect polarized lights, or the sun's angle, to figure out the location of home. Once the cat gets close, she picks her way through a familiar neighborhood to the right house. But remember, cats track down places, not people. If you move and leave the cat behind, she will not be able to find you.

- If she concentrates on the seal, she's pretty smart.

- If she figures out how to open it, she's a genius.

- If she falls asleep, she is either:

  a) not ready for cat college;

  b) very sleepy;

  c) very full, so she doesn't care about having some milk; or

  d) she has read this part of the book, and is faking you out.

Here, Kitty!

You can teach a cat to respond to the sound of her name and to come when you call her. Use food as the lure. Here's how:

- For some reason cats respond to sounds that end in "e" or "y." (Example: Kitty. So even if your cat's name is Thorndyke, call "Thorneee," or "Thorndyke, kittyyyy!")

- Don't use any other words except her name. Don't call, "Come on over here, my sweet Thorneee!" Just call the cat's name, or at most use, "Here, Thorndykeeee!" (or whatever way you want to use the name, as long as it ends in the "eeee" sound).

- If you call your cat just before you put down her food, she will soon associate her name with something good and come running when you call. If possible, always slip her a treat when she comes.

Who's crazy here? In the United States, superstitious people think a black cat means bad luck. In Great Britain, people think a black cat means good luck.

Testing Color Vision

Cats do see in color. Here's how to test your cat's color vision:

1 Get three medium-sized wood or cardboard boxes (all exactly the same size).

2 Paint one red, one blue, and one green.

3 While your cat watches, put a treat in the red box.

4 Now take the cat out of the room.

5 While she's gone, switch the location of the red box with the green box.

6 Bring the cat back into the room. Which box does she go to?

If she goes to the red box, her color vision is excellent. If she's puzzled, do the trick over again. If this takes more than three tries, forget it and go watch TV!

TV and Video

Cats love to watch television and videos. They follow the characters on the screen with great interest, because cats enjoy *movement.*

Watch TV with your cat and see what interests her the most. Do her eyes grow wide and move quickly? She may even jump at the screen to swat a certain image.

There are cat videos for sale in pet shops that show birds, fish, squirrels, or other cats. Get one to play for your cat when you have to leave her alone. You can also make a video for your cat. Tape her in action, or just tape the yard, with birds, bugs, swaying flowers or leaves, and other animals. She'll love it!

Cat Tricks with Photos, Mirrors, and Lights

Who Is That Cat?

Cats will also react to realistic still pictures and to photographs. Show your cat pictures from magazines and books, and see how she reacts. What does she do when you show her a cat? A dog? A bird or fish? Can she recognize a photo of you, another family member, or herself?

Mirror, Mirror

Some cats will stare in the mirror, fascinated by the image. They probably know it is their own reflection, but they can't figure out how it got there! Put your cat in front of a mirror and run your finger across the mirror. Does she leap for it, or does she arch and ask to be petted? If she leaps, she thinks the action is going on "inside" the mirror. If she arches, she knows it's you. Or maybe she knows both, but just wants you to stop playing and settle down!

Show your cat a small mirror that is just big enough for her face. How does she react? Does she attempt to kiss herself in the mirror? Does she seem startled? Does she get mad because there is another cat around?

Light-Catch

With you and your cat in a darkened room, beam the light from a flashlight on the wall. Let your cat adjust to it for a moment or two, then have the beam slowly inch its way up, then down, then across. Your cat will leap at the beam, "attack" it, and follow it. She knows it isn't alive . . . but this is a game, silly!

Some people think cats are "magical" because they seem to have ESP, or Extrasensory Perception. This is because the senses of a cat are very finely tuned. Cats feel vibrations we don't feel, and they hear sounds we can't hear. So if your cat jumps up and hisses at "nothing," she is reacting to noise you can't detect. And if you live in an earthquake region and she runs out of the house, she might be warning you to run, too.

Hide-and-Seek

Cats usually won't play hide-and-seek with you as the object, but they will allow you to hide something, and they will make a game of "seeking" it.

1 Show your cat a favorite toy, then you and your cat play with it for a few minutes.

2 Take the toy to another room, or outside, where the cat can't see you.

3 In the house, "bury" the toy under a blanket. Outside, you can bury the toy under some leaves or just hide it under a bush.

4 Bring the cat into the room, or outside near the spot where you hid the toy. She will probably look for the toy.

5 If she's puzzled, jiggle the blanket or poke the leaves to help her. You may have to take the toy out, show it to her, and bury it again so she can catch on to the game.

6 When she finds the toy, play with her as a reward.

Chapter 4

Games Cats Love

Cats enjoy games, provided their human pets adhere to the rules. Cats don't follow rules, but they expect you to do so. After all, you are only a human. Cats are special.

Back-and-Forth Swat

Exceptional cats will actually run after an object that you throw, and bring it back. Most often, however, they will "attack" it where it lands, and wait for you to send something else their way.

Cats like to pounce, pretending the object is a small animal. They may also swat it around.

If your cat retrieves with her mouth, she may think she's a dog. Most cats will retrieve with their paws: They will swat an object back to you, asking for a game of back-and-forth.

1 Bunch up a wad of paper into a ball.

2 Swat it lightly across a bare floor.

*C*ats do bring things to their owners, but usually it's not a toy. It's a dead bird, mouse, or other small unfortunate creature the cat has captured. The cat will plop this into your lap or leave it at the entrance to your home. Don't scold her; she is bringing you a *gift*. To a cat there is no greater way to say "I love you." Hunting for your gift is part of a cat's makeup (if she does love you), so scolding won't make her stop. Bury the poor gift and keep your cat so busy with games that she doesn't have time to go "shopping" for you.

3 The cat will swat it back, and keep up the game until: a) Your arm begins to snap; b) The paper ball shreds; c) The cat decides she would rather eat, and goes looking for her food dish.

Stair and Table Swat

Here are some variations on the back-and-forth swat game:

1 Use another bunched-up piece of paper or a Ping-Pong ball.

2 Starting at the top of the stairs, push the ball gently so it rolls down at least two steps.

3 Watch as your cat bounds down after the toy and swats it down the rest of the steps.

Now switch to a table:

1 Send the ball sliding over the table.

2 Does your cat grab it before it goes over the edge?

3 Put the toy at the edge of the table. Does your cat swat it over, or does she sit on the floor, looking up, waiting for the ball to be swatted down to her?

Sock-It-To-Me

In addition to pouncing and swatting, cats often enjoy wrestling with their "prey." They will grab an object with their front paws and kick it with their back paws, often while biting it as well.

We don't recommend that you let your cat do this with *you* . . . so try it with a pair of old socks instead.

1 Roll some old socks into a ball.

2 Scoot the sock-ball across the floor or dangle it in front of the cat.

3 Watch her grab the socks and wrestle with them.

4 Next time, ask her to wash the socks and put them in the drawer. (That *would* be a trick!)

Leap!

Cats are natural leapers, so most will take to this game very quickly.

1 Hold your cat's favorite toy at arm's length, about two or three feet above the cat's head.

2 Your cat will sit and study the situation. (She's thinking, "Do I go for it, or would I rather take a nap right now?")

3 She'll probably decide to go for it. Suddenly she will leap up, with paws extended, to grab the toy.

4 Don't jerk the toy up or away—play fair, and let her have it.

5 Let your cat enjoy her victory for a moment or two, then take the toy back and hold it even higher.

6 Keep raising the height of the toy, and thus the height of the leaps. You may be shocked at how high she can leap from a sitting position!

7 Continue until cat gives you a dirty look, which means, "I'm not going one inch higher!"

Cat Fishing (Not to be confused with catfish)

This is another activity that relies on your cat's natural leaping ability.

1 Get an old (or toy) fishing pole. If you don't have a pole, use a thin, long stick.

2 Tie a feather or light toy onto the pole with sturdy twine, as if the feather was the bait at the end of a fishing line.

3 Dangle the toy in front of the cat, and she will leap for it.

4 If you keep the toy enticingly beyond her reach, your cat will claw, bounce, dance, and grab for the toy.

5 Let her have the toy every once in a while, or she'll get frustrated and stalk off to watch "The Simpsons" on TV.

Safety tip: Don't leave the string out for your cat to play with when she is alone. Some cats will swallow string and choke.

D o cats really land on their feet? Not always. A cat is so agile that when she falls, the tail swivels in mid-air. That swivel puts the cat in position to land on all fours. A falling cat will also arch her back to absorb the shock of landing. If the cat has enough time to accomplish the swivel and arch, she may be all right. But many short-distance falls are fatal to cats. For your cat's safety, be sure windows are locked and screens and porch openings are securely closed.

Piggyback Rides

Cats love to snoop around, and there's no better way to do it than to ride on your shoulders so she can get a high-up view. Here's how to play cat piggyback (kittyback?):

1 Sit cross-legged on the floor and let your cat crawl all over you.

2 When she's comfortable with this, lure her onto your shoulders by wiggling your collar or placing a treat near your collar. Put her up there gently if she doesn't go by herself. Drape a towel around your neck first in case the cat accidentally claws you as she crawls around.

3 Sit still and let her stay on your shoulder for a few minutes, so she can determine that it's safe.

4 Now, get up slowly.

5 If your cat jumps off, start over. You probably went too fast.

6 When she's finally on your shoulders, walk around slowly and let her investigate pictures on the wall and peek into cabinets.

7 Try the same thing a little later. This time, put treats in cabinets so she gets a reward for peeking, or put treats on top of picture frames, on shelves, or other high places.

8 Pretty soon, she'll jump on your shoulders by herself.

9 If you've gotten this far, try putting on some slow music and dancing with your cat on your shoulders.

Paper Bag Bounce

If you don't believe cats are curious, try this activity. Not many cats can resist investigating a paper bag.

1 Put an empty paper bag (from the grocery store) on the floor, on its side, with the opening toward your cat.

2 Wait for your cat to crawl inside. If she doesn't go in right away, try tapping on the bag to get her attention.

3 When she's inside, make a scratching noise on the outside of the bag with a spoon or other object. The cat will follow the sound, and "answer" you by pawing at the spoon from inside.

4 Keep scratching at different spots on the bag. The bag will bounce as the cat quickly moves from spot to spot, following the noise.

5 For a variation on this game, poke five or six holes in the bag (before the cat goes inside!).

6 When the cat goes in the bag, stick the spoon through one of the holes. She will paw at the spoon.

7 Quickly withdraw the spoon, and poke it through another hole. Your cat will try to "capture" the spoon at each hole.

Got Ya!

Here's a great way to help your cat practice her pouncing:

1 Peek around a door at your cat.

2 Withdraw quickly when the cat sees you.

3 Peek around the door again. This time, the cat will try to sneak up on the door, then pounce. ("Got ya!")

4 The cat may pretend to be scared, and dash a few feet away. She's trying to coax you out from behind the door, so she can grab you and win the game ("Got ya again, dummy!")

Cats don't scratch furniture to sharpen their claws. They do it to exercise, or to mark their territory. To "make its mark," a cat picks its favorite chair, or a table in the sun, and scratches it to say "This is mine." A cat won't scratch furniture it doesn't like.

5 When you're exhausted, your cat may go to another door and wait, to entice you into just one more game.

Buried Treasure

Cats love to steal (uh . . . borrow) toys and other objects and bury them. Maybe this is a holdover from a feline's wild days in the desert, when the best way to hide a treasured object was to bury it in the sand. This game takes advantage of your cat's natural desire to dig.

1 Take your cat out to an area of yard where there is loose dirt or sand (make sure your parents don't mind if this area is dug up). Play with the cat for a while, using a favorite toy.

2 Let your cat watch you bury the toy a few inches down in sand or dirt. She will probably dig it right up.

3 The cat may then bury the toy in another spot, for you to dig up.

4 If this continues for a while, plant something nice in all those little holes you two have dug.

You can play this trick with your cat indoors, too. *No, do not bring sand or dirt indoors!* Merely use a sofa as your "dirt," hiding the toy under a cushion instead of burying it. Cats will stash objects under furniture, between bedsheets, or behind the TV.

Things You Can Buy for Your Classy Cat

Discount stores, pet shops, and novelty shops are filled with fun stuff for you and your cat. Here are just a few of the items you can buy:

- remote control mouse that you can send zooming across the floor with a controller disguised as a slice of Swiss cheese

- videotape of birds and fish called "Video Catnip"

- real catnip

- cat care books and magazines

- cat treats shaped like mice

- cat gymnastic sets

- novels with cats as the heroes

- cat movies such as "Homeward Bound," "Harry & Tonto," and "That Darn Cat"

- rubber stamps, stickers, photos, and binders, all depicting cats

- cat mugs or milk glasses

- picture frames for cat photos

- recordings of songs about cats, made by Garrison Keillor

- soothing selections of classical music to play for your cat, called "Classical Cats," which includes sounds of purring and contented meows

Great Toys from Everyday Objects

The best cat toys cost zero! Like toddlers, cats take great pleasure in turning everyday items into objects made for fun. Sometimes their wily ways result in a mess—as when toilet paper becomes a shredded blanket of white stuff for you to clean up—but you can avoid that. How? By keeping an eye out for simple household items that easily can be turned into kitty toys *before* the cat discovers them herself, and transforms them into kitty litter.

Toilet Paper and Tissues

Cats love the flimsy stuff, because it's easy to shred (be prepared for the cleanup).

1 Tear off some toilet paper and wad it into several little balls. Watch your cat make confetti.

2 Stuff an empty toilet paper roll with toilet paper. The cat will have a great time pulling the paper out and shredding it.

3 Yank tissues out of the box one by one, letting them float around the cat. She'll "dance" as she rushes to get each one.

4 Clean up the mess and pretend it never happened. The cat won't tell.

Tip

*C*ats have the best hearing in the animal world. It takes about two weeks after birth for a kitten to hear well, but once her hearing is developed a cat can hear and recognize her owner's footsteps hundreds of feet away!

Pencils

1 Let a pencil roll toward the edge of your desk while your cat watches. She will "help" it over the edge.

2 Once the pencil is on the floor, it becomes a rolling toy. The cat may even grab the pencil in her mouth and bring it back up on the desk, so she can push it over the edge again.

Rugs

1 Lift the edge of a rug and roll a ball or toy underneath it. Your cat will dive in after it.

2 Let the rug down a little, but don't bury the cat (she'll be frightened).

3 Prop the rug up with a stick or box. Your cat will dart in and out, rolling the toy as she goes.

Baskets

1 Fill a light wicker basket about halfway full with crumpled paper.

2 Rustle the paper to get your cat's attention.

3 Tip the basket over on its side. The cat will jump in and roll among the papers.

4 Scatter some papers next to the overturned basket. Does she push them back in—or scatter them some more?

5 If she pushes them back in, ask her to clean your room next.

Feathers

1 Tickle your cat's face or paws with a feather (you can pull one off a feather duster). She will swat at the feather.

2 Drop the feather from a few feet up, and she will jump to meet it, shake it, and scamper around with it.

3 If she can't make it "come alive" again on her own, she will drop it and wait for you to get the action going.

Towels

1 Roll a towel lengthwise.

2 Let your cat unroll it and drag it around.

3 Prop the towel up like a little tent (a large towel can be draped over a box or the lower part of some furniture). She will crawl through and explore it.

Cat owners in California claim their pets can "feel" when an earthquake is coming. Other owners say their cats know when an alarm clock is about to ring or can smell a leaking gas line. These people are probably right. Cats hear much better than humans—and they smell better, too! Their whiskers are also very sensitive to tiny air movements that humans cannot detect.

4 Pull a toy on a string through the "tent" for her to pursue.

5 Bunch the towel up and your cat will knock it apart.

6 After all this, your cat may claim the towel as her own and drag it to her sleeping place.

Pipe Cleaners

Cats love the fuzzy texture of pipe cleaners. You can buy a package of them at a hardware or drug store. Remember to put the pipe cleaners away after playing so your cat can't chew on them and choke when you're not watching.

1 Bend the pipe cleaners into different shapes and your cat will try to unbend them.

2 Roll them along the floor for her to chase and capture.

3 Shape several pipe cleaners into a ball. She will run after the ball and pull it apart.

4 Pipe cleaners bent into different shapes and suspended on a string will keep the cat enchanted for a long time.

Walnuts

1 Get four or five unshelled walnuts. Make sure they are big enough so that your cat won't swallow them and choke.

2 Put the nuts in an empty tissue box and tape over the opening.

3 Cut a hole just big enough for the cat's paw to get inside.

4 Rattle the box. She will stick in her paw and push the box around trying to get the nuts.

The term "scaredy-cat" comes from a cat's well-known habit of running away in the face of danger. Cats, however, are not cowards. They are just smart enough to know when to get away. A mother cat in New York named Scarlett went back inside a burning building five times to get her kittens and bring each one to safety, suffering terrible burns as a result. Scarlett and her kittens all survived. Her story shows cats are brave when they have to be!

Paper Bag Tunnel

1 Cut the bottoms off two paper bags. Put the bags together on their sides to create a tunnel. Your cat will go inside.

2 When she's in, wiggle a feather or pipe cleaner at one tunnel opening. She will try to grab the object and drag it inside her tunnel.

3 Pull the bags apart and see if she takes the toy from one bag to another.

The Suction-Cup Swing

1 Find a suction cup, string, and a lightweight toy.

2 Fasten the toy to a piece of the string.

3 Tie the other end of the string to the suction cup and stick the suction cup to the wall about two feet above the cat's head.

4 Give the toy a push. The cat will leap up for the toy as it swings along the wall.

Tip *An otherwise brilliant research scientist in San Diego became so fascinated with this toy that he stuck the suction cup on his forehead. He reports that the suction cup leaves a big red mark on your head when you try to pull it off, and "it hurts." Do not try to duplicate this research.*

Other Around-the-House Toys

Your cat will find plenty of other things to play with as she explores your home and yard. Here are some good additional around-the-house toys to try out on her:

- Empty thread spools

- Ping-Pong balls

- Drinking straws

Be careful; some around-the-house stuff is dangerous for your cat.

Don't give your cat soft rubber toys, because she'll shred them and swallow bits of the rubber. It's also bad for her to swallow buttons, beads, marbles, or other small items. Rubber bands can snap in her face. Anything with sharp or jagged edges, or anything made of glass, should be kept away from cats. Watch out for soft wood—it splinters—and keep her away from things painted with toxic paints. Licking mothballs, soap, room deodorizers, or detergents can make your cat very sick. Bug sprays or powders can kill your cat, and so can the leaves of poinsettias, philodendron, dieffenbachia, and some ivy plants. Keep your cat away from houseplants she might chew and swallow. Outside, just a few drops of antifreeze from the car can also be deadly.

Catnip is an herb, formally known as Nepeta Cataria. It is harmless, fun for most cats, and nonaddictive. If you get seeds from any large nursery or seed company, you can grow catnip at home in a clay pot.

Chapter 6

Other Things to Make for Your Cat

Because the cat knows you have been put on earth to make her life easier, why not get right to work? There is a bunch of fun stuff to make for your cat, and a great reward when you're done: the cat will actually use these things, proving that you are not just another ineffectual human.

Indoor Kitty House

Okay, she might decide not to use it, but most cats seem to like the cozy feeling of an enclosed space. And at least she'll know you care!

1 Get a sturdy, medium-sized cardboard carton.

2 Cut off the flaps and turn the carton upside down.

3 Cut out a small square for the door about three inches off the ground.

4 Write your cat's name above the door, and let her personalize it with her pawprint, made by dipping her paw in nontoxic paint and pressing gently next to her name (be sure to wipe off her paw immediately afterward).

5 Provide furnishings—a soft blanket and her favorite toy.

6 Place the house in a dimly lit corner where there is no human traffic.

Ladder Perch

Cats love to perch high above everyone else and look down at all those inferior beings below. This perch can be temporary or permanent (provided you have a parent's permission).

1 If you have a narrow but tall ladder for the house, place it against a corner wall or leading up to an empty shelf that is sturdy enough for your cat.

2 If you don't have a ladder, make one (with an adult helper) from a smooth plank of wood, with small paw-holds made of wooden blocks nailed to the wood every few inches.

3 Be sure the ladder or the wood is free of dirt and splinters.

4 Put a treat at the top of the ladder, and make sure that your cat sees you do this.

5 Watch your cat go up the ladder to get her treat. Once she's up, she'll probably stay there for a while to check out the view.

6 If the ladder leads to a top shelf, this could become her hangout.

7 The cat's perch can be just a few feet off the floor, or much higher if you prefer. Keep the perch at a height that feels safe and comfortable to you.

Windowsill or Tree Perch

Cats also like to hang out on windowsills—especially sunny ones—and if they are outdoor cats they will try to find a thick, low tree branch in the sun to serve as their perch. Here's how to make your cat's perch more comfortable. (Be sure to ask your parent's permission before enhancing the cat's windowsill or favorite tree.)

1 Let your cat pick her favorite window. It will probably be one that gets sunshine at least part of the day and has a lively view. (Cats are sun worshippers because they like to be warm, and they prefer views with people, cars, or other animals because movement interests them.)

Why do people say it's "raining cats and dogs?" The saying might have come from seventeenth-century England, when cats (and some dogs) were encouraged to prowl the rooftops hunting rats. When it rained, the animals slid off the roofs, and it looked like it was raining cats and dogs!

2 Get a sturdy wood plank that is slightly longer than the windowsill and wide enough for your cat to stretch out comfortably.

3 Be sure the wood is smooth; sand it if necessary.

4 Paint the wood with nontoxic paint the same color as the windowsill, wrap it in colorful fabric, or ask an adult to help you wallpaper it.

5 Attach two brackets on either side of the windowsill and lay the plank across them, so the plank is at the same height as the windowsill.

Mark Twain once said, "If man could be crossed with the cat, it would improve man but deteriorate the cat."

6 Attach the plank to the brackets with screws (you may need an adult's help for this). If the brackets are long enough, and sturdy enough, the plank may rest securely enough on top of them so you don't need to screw it down.

7 Put your cat's favorite cushion or blanket on top of the plank.

8 If you have an outdoor cat, pick a low tree branch and create the same type of perch for your cat in your yard. She'll enjoy a perch with a view of the door so she can watch the family coming and going. Include a cat ladder for easy access.

Tip You can create a cat "garden" just outside the window of the cat's indoor perch by planting trees or bushes that attract butterflies and installing a bird feeder (not on the window; birds won't get that close if they know a cat is nearby). If your cat goes outdoors, make sure the feeder is on a high pole so the cat can watch, but not catch, the birds.

Scratching Post

Unless your cat is declawed, she will love having her own scratching post. It will give her something else to play with, a way to stretch and exercise, and may even keep her from clawing the couch—for a while.

1 Take an old piece of carpet about two feet long and four feet wide and roll it into a long cylinder so that it is two feet high (carpet remnants are usually available at most carpet and department stores, and are quite inexpensive). Hold the roll together with masking tape.

2 Cut strips of carpet at the bottom of the cylinder so the strips can be attached to a platform of wood.

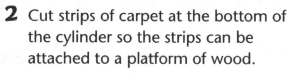

3 Ask an adult to help you staple the roll to the platform with a staple gun. The wood should be heavy enough to support the roll in an upright position and not topple over when the cat pushes against the roll.

4 You can also just nail some carpet to the wall (careful—pick a place approved by parents!).

5 Show your cat her post or wall carpet, and she'll happily scratch away.

6 You can also buy scratching posts in pet shops.

Cat Pillow

Because cats spend up to 20 hours out of every 24 hours sleeping, dozing, or resting, they enjoy soft pillows. Your cat will probably select several pillows as her favorites: one on the couch, one on a chair, and perhaps even the pillow from your bed!

You can make a pillow for your cat to encourage her to spend more time on her own resting place than on yours . . . but there are no guarantees!

1 Get a pillowcase that your parent no longer wishes to use.

2 Wash and dry it thoroughly.

3 Stuff it with clean, soft rags or old towels, making sure that the stuffing is loose enough so that your cat can punch it down when she wants a nap.

4 Sew the pillowcase closed.

5 If you're good at sewing, you can embroider your cat's name on the pillow.

6 Place the pillow atop one of your cat's favorite resting places.

7 A treat nestled in the center of the pillow will encourage your cat to use it, at least for the first time. If a cat uses a resting place and is comfortable there, she is likely to return.

Cat Clothing

Will cats wear clothes? Sure—for a little while. Usually, you can coax your cat into putting up with clothes long enough to get some adorable photos. (See Chapter 10.) Be sure to tie things loosely, and to remove everything as soon as you are finished . . . or she'll remember being uncomfortable in clothes, and there won't be a next time! Make a "clothing chest" from a box and have it handy so you can whip out the stuff when it's dress-up time. Here are some things a cat can wear:

- sunglasses (fasten with ribbon or string)

- doll or baby hats

- booties

- tiny T-shirts or frilly baby blouses

Cats can learn to recognize from 25 to 50 words. A cat will sometimes respond to a familiar word by looking up at you and opening her mouth as if to meow but making no sound. The sound is actually being produced, but not at a range that humans can hear. Your cat may be so convinced you're on her wavelength that she is "talking" to you in sounds only other cats can hear.

- ribbons around her neck

- baby sweaters

- animal clothing made especially for cats or small dogs, such as raincoats, booties, sweatshirts, and coats. These are available in many pet shops.

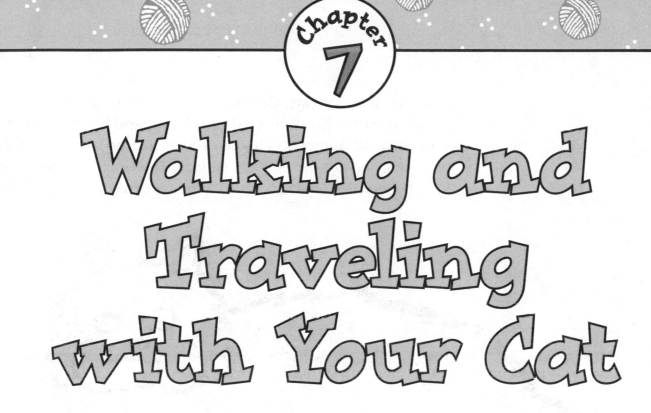

Chapter

7

Walking and Traveling with Your Cat

What? Take your cat for a walk? On a leash? Get real!

The reality is that cats *do* like to go for walks. They wear collars and halters, and take pretty readily to a leash.

Walks are good for cats. Cats enjoy fresh air and sunshine, love the attention usually given to a cat on a leash, and like to explore the neighborhood. Sometimes house cats will eat too much and snooze too much, and not get enough exercise. The result? A bored, sometimes hyperactive, and very fat cat. The cure may be a daily walk.

Doin' the Catwalk

It's better to walk with a *leashed* cat because she won't get lost or go zooming up a tree when you least expect it. All you need is a lightweight leash (made from cotton, nylon, or thin leather, for small dogs) and a harness.

Here's how to get started on your first walk:

1 Prepare your cat by putting the leash and harness in her favorite nap spot for several days before the walk. This helps her get used to the look, feel, and smell of the harness and leash.

2 Let her wear the harness in the house, on and off, for a few more days. If she tries to claw it off or seems unhappy, give her a treat the next time you put it on, so the cat will associate the harness with something good.

3 Attach the leash to the harness and let her drag it around until she's comfortable. (Don't forget the treat!)

4 Showtime! At first, when you go outside, let *her* walk *you*. Pick up the leash and follow wherever she wants to go. It is not necessary, however, to follow her up a tree. Don't jerk, pull, tug, or yell. Be a cool cat.

The fattest cat on record is Himmy, who lived in Australia and weighed almost 46 pounds. The fattest American cat, Gigi, weighed 42 pounds. Compare that to the average house cat weight of seven to nine pounds for a full-grown male and six to eight pounds for a female.

5 When the cat seems at ease, move in the direction *you* want to go, gently urging the cat with treats and encouraging words to come along.

Cat-walking tips:

- If the cat won't budge, or walks and stops suddenly, tug gently one time and quickly release. You may have to repeat this four or five times.

Collars or halters for your cat are available in pet stores. They range from simple, inexpensive models to very fancy types that cost a lot of money. If your cat is allowed outdoors, she should always wear a collar with her license tag attached to it. The tag should also display her name and your name, address, and telephone number so your cat can be returned to you if she gets lost. Ask your veterinarian for the best type of collar for your cat (some collars get caught on sharp objects, or they can strangle the cat). A harness is better for walking than a collar because it fits more securely and won't choke the cat.

- Before you venture out, make sure no threatening animals are around.

- Don't let anyone else take the leash until your cat is completely comfortable walking with you.

- Relax! The cat will eventually become a great walking companion.

Traveling with Your Cat

Now that she's a pro with a leash, your cat is ready to show off for others. It's also possible to take her on trips, because with a leash you can take her out of the carrying case and she will not be in danger of getting lost or hurt. Use the leash only when the place you're visiting is within easy walking distance. Otherwise, use a carrying case.

The Carrying Case

You can buy a carrying case in most pet shops. It should be large enough for your cat to stand up in, turn around comfortably, and stretch out. Firm cases are better than soft ones, because the soft ones tend to bend inward and the cat may feel as if the case is collapsing around her. The case should open from the top and have a front screen or mesh so your cat can see what's going on. Line the bottom of the case with your cat's favorite blanket or pillow, and put in one or two of her toys. No water or food; it will spill.

Give your cat a treat every time you put her in the case, so she doesn't resist. Some cats will struggle when you try to put them in the case, so take your time, speak gently to your cat, and never shove or force her in. If she resists after two or three times, rethink your travel plans. She may be much happier at home, or even in a kennel.

English-speaking people love cats so much that they have incorporated that fondness into the language. When you want to say a person is great, he or she is "the cat's pajamas," or "the cat's meow." Something that looks terrific is "the cat's whiskers."

Keep your cat's harness and leash on in the case, so you don't have to put them on when she gets out, and thus risk her getting away. Make sure to have a firm grasp on the leash before you let her out of the case.

Other Travel Tips

Test your cat's willingness to travel by putting her in the case and having your parent drive her around the neighborhood. If she cries or seems agitated, she may dislike the movement of the car or the insecurity of leaving home. Wait a few days and try again. This time put a treat in her carrying case and give her another one en route. If she is still uncomfortable, she is probably a homebody, not a traveler. Cats have an amazing sense of balance, so they don't get carsick as readily as dogs. Most cats, however, hate cars. They associate the car with a trip to the vet, or they get very, very bored just driving around.

- Never allow your cat to be in a car without being confined to her case. A cat that is loose in a car is a danger to herself and to the driver.

- Don't take your cat on trains or planes unless the trip is unavoidable. In some cases she may have to travel in the baggage compartment, which is frightening and possibly unsafe.

Ancient Egyptians worshipped cats as gods. During the Middle Ages, people thought cats were witches. Now, cats outrank dogs as the number one pet in the United States.

- Call ahead to make sure the hotel where you plan to stay accepts animal guests. If you are visiting friends or relatives, ask their permission to bring your cat. They may have a family member who is allergic to cat dander, or a resident dog who enjoys chasing or biting cats.

- Keep your cat in only one room of the house or hotel where you're visiting, so she can't get lost.

- Bring along her favorite toys, food, and food and water dishes, plus her litter box and a supply of litter. Don't forget any necessary medications.

Home Alone

Leaving the cat home while you travel? No problem. Cats have a strong sense of place and are happiest in familiar surroundings, so your cat will probably prefer this to being bounced around from place to place.

Cats can safely stay home alone for about three days, if a neighbor or friend comes to change the litter box and provide fresh food and water daily. Never leave a cat home alone for more than 24 hours without a cat-sitter checking on her. There are professional "critter sitter" services in most large cities that provide an experienced professional who will visit your cat daily, feed her, change the water in her dish, provide fresh litter, and even play with her so she is not lonely. You can find reputable sitters through your veterinarian, the local Humane Society, or some pet shops.

If you must leave your cat in a boarding kennel, make sure it's quiet, clean, and doesn't cater excessively to dogs (their yapping will drive her nuts). Visit the facility before you board your cat there and check out the size of the cage where she will live, its proximity to other animals, the cleanliness of the kennel, and whether the people there seem genuinely fond of cats.

Tricky Cats

Who says cats don't do tricks? Cats are original and highly creative tricksters, inventing games to play with and on their owners, and tricks to do that will amuse the people they love.

Just like the big cats who jump through hoops in the circus, your little cat can learn a variety of tricks. If you want a tricky cat, remember these three *absolute* rules:

- Always reward your cat with her favorite treat immediately after her performance.

- Never shout at your cat, hit her, or force her to do anything.

- Let her stop as soon as she wants to, and try again tomorrow.

Roll Over

1 Push your cat gently down on her side and say "Roll."

2 After a few times the cat will lie down on her own.

3 Roll her over very gently, giving her a treat when she rolls.

4 Reward her, and she'll roll over on her own when you say "Roll."

Jumping

You already know that cats are great jumpers. Here's how to turn that ability into a trick that will really get attention (this is how big circus cats are often trained):

1 Put three or four stools or low-back chairs in a circle (stools are best).

2 Put your cat on one of the stools.

3 Show her a treat, and put it on the stool closest to her. She will jump to the stool to get her reward.

Socks, the White House cat, doesn't know many tricks but still gets one million letters per year. Socks was given to Chelsea Clinton by her piano teacher. Her litter box is kept in the office of the White House engineer.

4 Put another treat on the next stool and she'll keep jumping.

5 Try holding a hoop between the stools. See if she'll jump through the hoop to get to the treat on the next stool.

Great Britain's Graham Thomas Chipperfield teaches lions and tigers circus tricks as lead animal trainer for Ringling Bros. and Barnum & Bailey. Chipperfield uses the natural talents of the big cats in a jumbo-sized version of the jumping trick. He says the key to success with cats is "respect for the animals." What gives him the most trouble, adds Chipperfield, is "interacting with my human coworkers."

Trick tip: Many cats will think up tricks of their own. Why? To get your attention, of course. Watch your cat. If you praise her when she does something you think is cute or funny, she'll do it again! And again! And again!

Cat Pool

This trick has nothing to do with swimming. Think billiards—as in knocking balls around with a long stick, hoping to pop them into a corner pocket. After you teach her this trick, your cat will be a pro.

If you have a real pool table, you're set. If not, with a little tape, a large cardboard box, and four old socks, you can make one.

Making the pool table:

1 Turn the cardboard box on end so it makes a stiff, sturdy table.

2 Cut the tops off the socks so you can use the bottoms as corner pockets.

3 Tape or tack the pockets to each corner of the box.

Now you're ready for kitty pool, cat billiards, or cat-swat:

1 Use an actual billiard ball, a small rubber ball, or any small, heavy ball.

2 First, show your cat how a ball rolls on the ground. Reward her when she swats or rolls it by herself.

Trick tip: If your cat seems wary of the pockets, put a treat inside them.
Another tip: If she seems wary of the balls, rub them in cat food and let dry.
Just one more tip: If cat food doesn't work, rub the balls in catnip.

3 Now roll the ball slowly on top of the box. If she jumps up and joins right in, reward her. If not, coax her up on the box with a treat.

4 Start rolling the ball to see if she swats at it. Each time she hits the ball, give her a treat.

5 When she gets the ball in a pocket, add praise to the treat.

Now you have a pool-playing cat! How many times can she get the ball in a pocket in the space of three minutes? Can she beat you at this trick?

Natural Cat Tricks

Cats do many things naturally that become tricks if you simply encourage the cat's behavior. Here are some natural tricks you'll enjoy:

1 Cats love to crawl or jump on your book, newspaper, or magazine when you're reading. (The cat does this to say, "Hey! Don't read, pay attention to *me* instead!") Get a cat magazine and open it to a page with a photo of a cat. Rub some catnip on the page and let it dry. Then put the magazine where the cat can easily jump to it. She will probably go through the magazine until she finds the catnip-marked page. If you mark

The famous writer Mark Twain had a cat named Tammany who loved to play with her kittens on top of Twain's pool table. One of the kittens crawled into a corner pocket. Later, Twain tried to play pool. He shot a ball that came near the pocket where the kitten was hiding, and a little paw shot out and scooted the ball in another direction. From then on, said Twain, the kitten watched and "won" many games!

the page just before friends come to visit, you can dazzle them with a cat who can obey when you say "Find the photo of another cat!"

2 Some cats enjoy batting at the screen when you're playing computer games. Find a simple game that features an object going from side to side or up and down on the screen. If your cat paws at the object, following its pattern, give her a treat. Soon you may have a cat that will expertly mimic the pattern of the game as you play.

3 Young cats and kittens often have fun sliding on slick floors when running after toys, or just sliding for the fun of it. Select a toy that slides easily, and see if your cat slides after it. If she catches the toy, encourage her to keep sliding with it by giving both her and the toy a gentle push. If she complies, give her a treat. She may then slide the toy around the floor on her own. Now you have a cat in training for ice hockey!

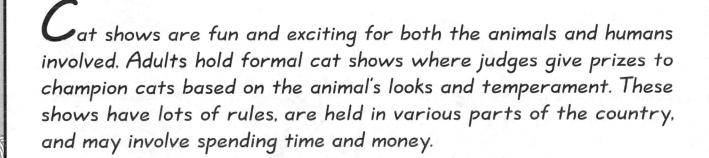

Cat Shows

Cat shows are fun and exciting for both the animals and humans involved. Adults hold formal cat shows where judges give prizes to champion cats based on the animal's looks and temperament. These shows have lots of rules, are held in various parts of the country, and may involve spending time and money.

Formal Cat Shows

Formal shows are often open to children and their cats. Some cat associations have "Junior Memberships" that help kids learn what is involved in entering a formal show. Ask about this when you contact the Cat Fanciers' Association. (See page 91 for their phone number.)

Here's what happens at a cat show:

1 Cats and their owners come from all over the country to be judged.

2 The owners wash and groom their cats so the animals look terrific. Some owners even "polish" their cats after brushing with a special chamois cloth to bring out the shine in the fur. (You can make your cat's coat look glossy by stroking her fur gently with a piece of silk or velvet fabric.)

3 Cats and owners wait their turn to be judged. While they wait, the owners chat about cats, groom their animals, and show them off. The cats rest in special show carriers, some of which are decorated as fancy bedrooms, jungle lairs, lion dens, castles, or mansions. Sometimes the carriers are just as much fun to see as the cats!

4 Judges look at the cat's head shape, body shape, fur, and many other physical attributes. They also check to see if the cat is good-natured and easy to handle.

5 Lots of people who don't have cats in the show come just to look. They walk around and peek into the carriers or ask permission to pet the cats. Some owners also sell kittens and older cats at these shows.

Unofficial Shows

Not all cat shows are fancy official affairs. Festivals, fairs, celebrations, and local gatherings also may have cat shows as part of the fun. Watch your neighborhood newspapers for such shows, or call your veterinarian or Humane Society. It's a great way to meet other people who love cats!

- Unofficial shows are open to everyone, and to all types of cats.

- They usually don't cost anything to enter.

- You may win prizes for yourself and your cat, such as free cat food, medals, tickets to a movie or show, or animal supplies.

- You can find out about clubs for cat owners at these shows.

- An unofficial show is great for finding out what types of cats

If your cat has a pedigree it may be eligible for a formal cat show. For information, write to The Cat Fanciers' Association, Inc., P.O. Box 1005, Manasquan, New Jersey, 08736-0805 (telephone 908-528-9797).

other people have. It also gives you a chance to talk about any questions or problems you may have concerning your cat. You can learn a lot—and have a great time—at unofficial cat shows.

The first cat show was probably the one at St. Giles Fair, in England, in 1598. Obviously nobody was very excited, because it took 273 years before another recorded show was held!

Create Your Own Show

Here are some ideas for a cat show that you can hold in your basement, den, or yard:

- **Fattest or Biggest Cat** Most cats weigh from 7 to 9 lbs. But there may be a muscle-cat in the neighborhood; this show will find him or her!

- **Best-Dressed Cat** Since many cats will let their owners dress them in everything from bonnets to booties, why not hold a contest to see which cat can come in the best costume?

- **Most Colorful Cat** There are few cats that are entirely one color; most have a range of fur colors in their coats. This show will net a prize for the cat with the most colors in its fur. All you have to do is count! (You can also have a contest for the fewest colors.)

You can probably come up with plenty of other ideas for holding a cat show. The show can be part of a party, or a reason for a party in itself! It's a fun way to get together with your friends and their cats.

How to Organize Your Own Cat Show

1 Ask your parent's permission to have the show. Then, with adult help, create a flyer that announces "Judy's Cat Show" or whatever name you'd like to give it. The flyer should list the date, time, place, and reason for the show, such as "To find the biggest cat in our neighborhood" or just "For cats and their owners on our street to get together and have fun."

2 Distribute the flyer to family, friends, and neighbors.

3 Have simple refreshments such as pretzels and soft drinks for the people; water and treats for the cats.

4 Ask your local pet shop if it would like to donate prizes, such as cat food, a fancy collar, or gift certificates for winners. It's great advertising for the shop. Ask your veterinarian, too.

*D*id you know that your cat's front paws probably have five toes, but the back ones only have four? Some cats have six or seven front toes. At a cat show, see if you can spot some many-toed cats.

5 Provide a table or big box on which cats can be judged.

6 Make sure there's plenty of room for people to put their cat carriers.

7 Ask some adults or older kids to be the judges.

8 Wrap up little candy packages and cat treats in tin foil and tie them with colorful ribbons, to be used as prizes for each contestant. That way, every kid and every cat gets something to take home, and everyone feels like a winner!

Chapter 10

Smile and Say "Meow!"

People who are owned by cats almost immediately become addicted to taking photos of their felines. Cats realize this, and assume a variety of poses guaranteed to keep you rushing to the store for more film: They roll on their backs and look at you upside down; they curl into little balls of fluff; they peek out of a basket; and they pretend to fall asleep inside your shoe.

There is only one thing you can do to cope with all this charm: Take a picture!

National Public Radio personality Garrison Keillor says "Cats are intended to teach us that not everything in nature has a function."

How to Take Cat Photos

1 Your best bet is to photograph the cat outdoors or in a well-lit room. Cats don't like flashes. Cameras don't like the dark.

2 Use a fast speed film (400 ASA).

3 Try sitting-still photos before you go for action shots. They're easier, and will give you practice in handling both the camera and the cat.

4 Keep it *very* simple at first. No costumes (yet) or mood shots.

5 When you have had the film developed, study your photos and ask yourself, "What do I like about this? What do I dislike?" Then you'll know what to do next time.

Best Times to Take Photos

- Right after the cat eats, and is content

- When she grooms herself after the meal (great paw-rubbing-face shots)

- Just as she s-t-r-e-t-c-h-e-s after her nap

- As she begins to play, not when she's ready to call it quits

About 140,000 pounds of catnip are sold yearly in the United States and Europe. Most of it is grown by a company in Maryland called Cosmic Catnip.

- When she's curious about the camera, but not afraid of it

- As she stares at a new toy or is attracted by some movement

- When catnip makes her silly, sleepy, or both

- When she says you can take the photo, and not a moment before

What's the Angle?

A good cat photo is any one that is successfully developed. A *great* photo uses inventive camera angles and bold closeups.

- Crouch down or squat when you're shooting, so you get a cat's-eye view.

- Put the cat on a table or other elevated object so she's at your level.

- Move in as close as possible so the cat's image fills the frame.

- Don't include background unless it's an important part of the story you want to tell with your picture. (If you want a shot of your cat curled up with the teddy bear, the bear is your only background, but if you want a shot of the cat alone, don't include the couch or whatever else she's on.)

- Sit cross-legged on the floor with the camera and put a treat right on your shoe. Take your photo as the cat comes toward the treat, with her eyes wide in anticipation and her tail up.

- Put a treat on top of the camera (make sure the cat knows it's there) and get the photo very close up as she reaches for the treat.

- Keep those treats handy! Models don't work for free.

What to Do with the Photos

- Create a table-top display of framed photos of your cat in different poses and situations.

- Blow up the best shots as posters for your room or use them on holiday greeting cards.

- Send photos to family and friends, or give framed photos as birthday gifts.

The human most often compared to a cat in looks is actress Michelle Pfeiffer. And many kids think that Jerry Seinfeld looks like a horse!

- Mail the really great photos to your local newspaper (make sure that the cat's name and your name, address, and telephone number are on the photo).

- Scan in the photo on your computer, or have several of them made into a nifty screen saver.

- Enter the photo in cute pet contests (watch your newspaper or a cat magazine for these).

- Put a photo on your stationery.

Cat Photo Contests

You can get together with friends who have both cats and cameras, and make up contests such as these:

- cutest cat photo

- guess my name (take photos of cat with props to suggest her name)

- best funny caption for a cat photo (for example, a cat peeking out of a basket could be captioned "Basket Case")

- wackiest costume

- best photo of cat caught in mid-air (action shot)

- photo most guaranteed to put you to sleep (best sleeping shot)

- nutty kitten shot (best photo showing kitten doing something silly—you won't have to wait long to get the photo)

- dual shots of owners and their cats, for a Look-Alike contest (you decide which people look most like their cats, or which cats look most like their people)

Photo Books

Once you've accumulated a hefty collection of cat photos, starting with kittenhood, you can make the following types of scrapbooks with them:

- **My Cat's Life.** Told in photos, from the time she was a kitten to now, with each set of photos documenting another phase of growth

- **Cat Joke Book.** Dumb cat jokes (are there any other kind?) next to photos that best illustrate the jokes

- **Cat Cartoons.** Cat cartoons and funny drawings from newspapers and magazines, cut out and pasted next to photos showing your cat doing similar things

- **Family Album.** Photos of your cat with various family members

- **Me and My Cat.** Just the two of you, through the years

- **Cat Wisdom.** Pithy sayings about cats (get them from the encyclopedia, the Internet, books of quotations, newspapers, magazines, and cat magazines) pasted next to the photo of your cat that best illustrates the saying

Did you know? Animals do react to photos. Cats like to look at photos of themselves (what else?) and will purr at photos of their owners, hiss at dog photos, and drool at photos of food.

Chapter 11

Water Cats

The two words water and cat aren't supposed to go together. But like so many other things about cats, their like—or dislike—of water is a mystery. Some cats won't go near anything liquid. Others will dive right into a pool with you, and splash like a happy kid.

Go figure.

Cats got a reputation for disliking water because many of today's breeds are descended from the wild felines of the Libyan desert, and thus instinctively shy away from being wet. Another reason why cats avoid water is because their coats get soggy easily. Cat fur makes good insulation but a bad raincoat.

On the other paw, cats do need plenty of clean, fresh water to drink, and they are drawn to ponds, puddles, and other natural sources. Indoor cats like to play with water and don't mind splashing around if you introduce them gently to the bathtub, sink, or water toys.

Just don't get your cat soaked. Anybody who does that is a drip.

Catch-the-Drop

Cats are fascinated by kitchen sinks. From the cat's-eye view down on the floor, there's always *something* going on up near the sink—and it's usually good. Humans go to sinks to prepare food, and the clatter of dishes is bound to make any cat curious.

That's why you'll probably see your cat bounce up on the sink, anxious to sniff around and figure out what's cookin'. When she's up there, she'll be interested in the water pouring out of the faucet. She's probably thinking "What is that stuff, anyway? Where does it come from, and where does it go? How can I get some?"

Your cat's natural curiosity can easily be turned into a water game called catch-the-drop. Here's how:

1 Let your cat jump up on the sink, or lure her up with a treat.

2 Open the faucet just enough to start a steady drip-drip-drip.

3 Splash your finger through the drips to show your cat that it's harmless and fun. She may mimic you with her paw.

4 Let her catch the drips.

5 After a little while, turn off the faucet. She will be puzzled and do one of the following:

- Look up into the faucet to see if there's another drip coming (resist the temptation to open the faucet now and splat her

Abraham Lincoln found three stray cats soaking wet on a Civil War battlefield. He dried them off and took them home to live with him at the White House.

in the face. It may be funny for a second, but your cat will lose trust in you and probably hate water from that moment on)

- Poke at the drain to see if the water will come out of there

- Call her mother and complain about stupid human inventions

Tip

Never play any trick on your cat that will cause her to lose trust in you. A cat can't love someone she distrusts.

Spin the Bottle

This was the name of a popular kissing game in the 1950s. Now it's a game for cats (kisses optional).

1 Fill a plastic bottle half full with water, and let your cat watch you do this.

2 Cap or cork the bottle tightly.

3 Put the bottle on a bare floor and spin it around. The cat will go after the bottle and keep it spinning, fascinated by the way the water sloshes around inside.

4 Now roll the bottle. The cat will keep it rolling.

5 If she bites into the bottle and it springs a leak, find another bottle!

Want a neat "pet" for your pet? Get her a toy fish. Many toy shops sell realistic looking tropical fish in sealed bowls. Your cat will spend many happy hours staring at her fish as it swims and bobs in the bowl. To keep the cat safe, be sure the bowl is too heavy for the cat to tip over and that it cannot be pried open.

Bathtub Peek-A-Boo

Introduce your cat to the bathtub, to show her how much you like it. For the first introduction, you might just let her watch as you take a bath. Here's what to do next:

1 Bring along your cat's favorite waterproof toy when you are ready for a bath. Bring the cat into the bathroom.

2 After filling the tub and getting in, put the toy on the tub ledge. This will lure the cat over to the tub.

3 Sink down in the water and remain still. The cat will wonder where you've gone and may put her front legs on the tub to look over at you.

4 Pop up and say hello. She'll scamper away as if startled (probably only to make you feel guilty), then quickly return.

5 Repeat until: **a)** You become soggy and crinkled **b)** The cat becomes soggy and crinkled **c)** You both become soggy and crinkled **d)** You remember you went into the tub to get clean, not to get soggy and crinkled playing with a cat.

Tub Toss

Here's how to get your cat closer to the tub:

1 While you're in the tub, gently drop the cat's toy in, too.

2 Scoot it across the water. The cat may reach in and try to grab it with one paw. Let her have it; this will encourage her to try again.

3 Put the toy back in the water and splash the toy lightly. Does the cat try to mimic you and splash the toy with her paw?

4 Make bubbles or very small splashes near the toy, encouraging the cat to investigate.

5 Don't be surprised if she perches on the tub ledge or even joins you in the tub.

The superstitious Pilgrims took cats along on their journey to the New World for good luck. They believed anyone who drowned a cat on the journey would be cursed—and would drown too.

6 Do not, however, pull the cat into the water, because felines have been known to immediately transform themselves into great white sharks when involuntarily soaked by their owners. Nobody knows what happened after that, because no owners survived to testify. (Also, see the tip on trust.)

Shower Power

Your cat also may be interested in checking out the shower, and might even join you for a while.

1 Take one or two of your cat's waterproof toys with you to the shower, plus a pipe cleaner or some other flexible item you can manipulate.

2 Bring your cat into the bathroom with you. When you go into the shower, let her wait just outside the curtain. The sound of running water will make her curious, and she may try to peek inside. Some cats actually step into the shower, and if the water stream is gentle, they enjoy the spray (but not the soap).

3 If your cat stays outside the shower, slide the pipe cleaner just about an inch beyond the curtain or shower door, and attract the cat's attention by making the pipe cleaner "crawl" up the wall. The cat will paw the pipe cleaner, or jump up to get it.

4 Keep sliding the pipe cleaner, this time in and out of the shower. The cat may follow the pipe cleaner into the shower.

5 Now do the same with a toy. If the cat seems wary, peek out of the shower and gently call her name, to show her that it's only you in there under the spray!

"WADING" INTO CAT INFORMATION

*T*here is an ocean of cat information on the Web, in books, and in newspapers, magazines, and newsletters. Here's a sampling of what you can fish around for, and net, as you troll for facts. You'll get hooked on one of these:

- *The Catnip Newsletter.* An eight-page monthly. P.O. Box 420014, Palm Coast, Fla., 32142, Telephone 800-829-0926

- *Cats Magazine.* One Purr Place, P.O. Box 420236, Palm Coast, Fla., 32142, Telephone 904-445-2818

- *Cat Fancy Magazine.* P.O. Box 52864, Boulder, Colorado, 80322, 970-666-8504

- *CompuServe* (800-848-8199) and *America Online* (800-386-5550); both have pet forums and information on cats

- *Cat Owner's Newsgroup on the Web.* rec.pets.cats

- *Catz, Your Computer Petz.* http://www.pfmagic.com

Chapter 12

Playtime at Bedtime

Mature cats spend about 60 percent of their time sleeping. Kittens are asleep almost 90 percent of the time! Depending on her age, your cat will be in dreamland from 16 to 20 hours each day.

Next to hitting the sack, your cat's idea of a great time is to play before she falls asleep. There are some great games you and your cat can enjoy with little more than the same stuff you'd normally use during bedtime: sheets, pillows, and blankets.

While they sleep, cats move their paws, twitch their whiskers, and wiggle their ears. This suggests that cats—like dogs and humans—also have dreams. But nobody knows what cats dream about!

Puffed-Up Sheets

Part One

1 Clear off the bed, removing the blanket as well so there's only the sheet spread smoothly over the bed.

2 Let your cat get up on the bed.

3 Gently pull the sheet so the cat is "riding" on it. She will roll and scamper, trying to figure out how the sheet is moving.

Part Two

1 Let your cat stay at one side of the sheet, or off the sheet entirely, as you stand at the side of the bed.

2 Gently make the sheet billow, or puff up. The cat will pounce wherever the sheet billows, thinking there is something underneath.

Part Three

1 Let your cat crawl under the sheet.

2 Gently billow the sheet on top of her. She will "attack" the sheet as it comes down.

Batty Blanket

Cats obviously think every blanket they see has been put there just for them—because they immediately assume ownership. If the blanket is small, the cat is likely to drag it to her favorite perch or to a sunny spot on the floor, so she can sunbathe in style. If the blanket is too big, the cat will scrunch it into a lumpy mess that's just right for her reclining form. If there's a favorite or expensive blanket in the house, tuck it out of sight, because an exposed blanket is fair game for any self-respecting cat.

Blankets also make great cat toys. Here's a game that transforms your blanket into a plaything for you and your cat—and transforms those few boring moments before bed into a happy romp:

Tip

Don't encourage your cat to stalk and pounce on your toes without the protection of a blanket between you and her sharp claws and teeth. Ouch!

116

Part One

1 Put your cat up on the bed.

2 Get under the covers.

3 Wiggle your toes under the blanket, trying to make scratching noises as you do so. The cat will stalk your toes. Then she will pounce on your toes, pretending they are prey.

Part Two

1 Make a tunnel out of your blanket by lifting it in the middle and letting the folds of the blanket hold up the lifted part.

2 Stick the front of your body in at one end of the tunnel.

3 Let your cat find the other end. She will: a) stick the front of her body in, too; b) crawl through and lick your face; c) decide you're nuts and go to sleep.

Part Three

1 Pull one of your cat's toys through the tunnel on a string. She will crawl through after it.

2 Hide the toy in the tunnel, and watch as she hunts it down.

Good Night, Kitty

When your cat is ready for sleep, don't try to force her into playing some more. Sleep-deprived cats get cranky, ill-tempered, and even sick.

Nighttime seems to be danger time for outdoor cats. This is when they are most likely to get lost or stolen. If you can't keep your cat indoors at night, provide her with a safe, warm hideaway next to the house or garage that she can crawl into to escape roaming dogs, other cats, or human catnappers.

Whether it's a blanket, sofa cushion, or your tummy, cats getting ready to lie down on something for a nap often will knead it for several minutes before they snooze. Kneading helps the cat relax. It also is a sign of affection when a cat kneads a human. This is one way kittens ask their mothers for attention—and it's also an attention-getting device cats use on humans.

When cats become irritated with their owners for leaving them alone too long, they may go into the bedroom and pull blankets off their owners' beds. Cats seem to know the blanket and the owner are intimately connected.

If you have to leave your cat for a few days—or if you notice she gets lonely when you're gone just for a few hours during the day—a blanket with your scent on it will comfort her. Just buy an inexpensive blanket, or get an old but clean one that you can give to the cat. Sleep with the blanket for a night or two. The blanket will retain your scent, so that when you give it to the cat she will feel close to you and be a lot less lonely.

Top Ten Ways Cats Make Themselves Useful

Some people say cats are useless critters who play, sleep, and eat . . . and don't earn their keep. These misguided souls have no clue how hard cats work for their human owners. The next time somebody asks why you have a cat, assume a smug expression and rattle off these top ten uses for a feline pet:

1 Cats keep the mouse population within reasonable limits, although not all cats are mousers. The best mouse chaser in the world was Mickie, who worked in an English grocery store from 1945 to 1968. During that time Mickie caught 22,000 mice.

2 Cats visit hospitals to cheer and distract sick people. To volunteer your cat, contact Pet Partners, 289 Perimeter Road East, Renton, Washington, 98055-1329, telephone 206-226-7357.

3 Many therapists keep cats in the room to calm psychiatric patients.

4 Studies show that a person's blood pressure can be lowered just by petting a cat.

5 Cats are living works of art. In a Connecticut art gallery, pedestals for several resident cats are set up next to paintings so the cats can climb up and pose as art.

6 Cats are used in ads to sell everything from cereal to shoes. Tony the Tiger sells Kellogg's Frosted Flakes, for example, and Cat's Paw shoe soles tell a customer the shoe won't slip.

7 People don't need alarm clocks when they have a cat. A loud "Meow!" will remind them that it's time to get up and make breakfast.

8 Greeting card manufacturers use photos and drawings of cats to adorn birthday cards and other items.

9 Who needs heavy socks when a cat is around to warm your feet? They also function as lap-warmers, shoulder-warmers, tummy-warmers, and anything-else-they-can-lie-on warmers.

10 Cats inspire books like this one. What else could you possibly read that would be so useful?